About the Author

Kaushik Sen, has been working in the financial markets since 1995. He completed his MBA Degree, with finance as specialisation, in First class, from Pune University. He has worked as Area Manager at Bonanza Portfoilio Limited (A stock broking firm) for a brief period. He has also studied technical analysis and fundamental analysis and has been stock market analyst and was also a member of Association of Technical Market Analysts (ATMA).

Dedicated to my Family Members and Team Members

Disclaimer

Please note that the facts and figures mentioned in the book are based on the latest information available at the time of publishing. Since they could change with time, readers should verify the information before taking any financial decision.

Also note that not all investments covered in this book maybe suitable for every investor. Investment needs depend totally on individual situations and this book in no way recommends one investment option over the other. Readers are requested to make their own investigations and seek appropriate professional advice before opting for any of the investment options mentioned.

While due care has been taken in compiling the information for the book, we do not guarantee that the content, recommendations and analysis are complete and accurate. The author and publisher do not accept any responsibility or liability, whatsoever, for any error, omission, opinion or misrepresentation of information, however it may have occurred, and disclaim any liability to any person or group for the consequences of any decisions based on the contents of this book.

Acknowledgements

I wish to express my gratitude to all the people who have supported me in my career.

I would like to thank my clients, team members, for supporting and motivating me to continue my good work, and acquire my experiences, needed to write this book.

Also, I would like to thank my teachers and faculties, who taught me in my schools and colleges, for giving me such high level of knowledge and understanding, to be able to pen down my thoughts.

This book is reflection of my experiences, gained while working in the financial markets since 1995. And this could not have been possible without the support of my clients and distributors.

Contents

Introduction

In 1995, just after completing my class 12, I had joined the financial industry by taking up agency of Life Insurance Corporation of India. My sole objective at that time was to gain some experience, while continuing my studies. Never had I imagined at that time, that I would find my full time profession in the financial markets.

While working in the financial markets, I had the opportunity to meet and interact with lot of professionals working in the financial markets. Some were working part-time, and some full-time. What I understood was that there were lot of gaps in the knowledge and awareness level of the financial advisers. Some of them came as they had no other option. Some of them came as their father, grandfather were into this business. But many of them did not realise the need of knowledge about financial markets to be successful in this profession.

So this book is written to educate the financial advisers and distributors, so that they can guide their clients well.

* 1 *

Financial Distribution Business

Financial distribution business refers to the distribution of financial products like loans, mutual funds, insurance, loans & so on.

Theoretically, financial distribution business refers to the selling of financial products to clients and end-users. Financial distributors act as intermediaries between the principal company and the client.

Practically, the financial distribution business includes much more than the selling of financial products. It involves need analysis, advisory and after-sales support, apart from upfront sales.

A client wants to invest in mutual funds. There are various companies offering different types of schemes. The official role of a financial distributor is to sell one, two, or three schemes to the client, collect the cheque from the client, and submit the cheque to the company. But the big question is that who is going to decide, which scheme is good for the client, whether the equity scheme is good for the client, or the debt scheme is good for the client. And herein comes the role of advisory and creation of awareness.

A financial distributor is expected to explain all the advantages and disadvantages of various schemes to the client. On the basis of the knowledge imparted by the financial distributor, the client is expected to decide which scheme is best suited for him or her. And this entire exercise constitutes financial distribution business.

Unfortunately, in India, it does not happen so. Either the client decides blindly posing to know everything. Or the distributor or agent, decides the scheme, mostly depending on which fund gives him or her the best commission or margin. Or the client asks the distributor or agent to decide on the behalf of the client, out of blind faith on the distributor/agent. But these are not correct practises. I only hope that these thought processes of client and distributors, and the way of doing financial distribution business in India, changes in the coming future.

Advantages of Financial Distribution Business

A job requires employability, which means qualification, aptitude, and skills to clear the interview. A business requires inevitability along with risk appetite and business acumen.

But financial distribution business does not require a high degree or extensive investment. The financial distribution business revolves around the practical skills of the financial distributor and levels of contact base of the distributer.

Ideally, in a job, higher qualifications normally lead to a higher salary. Similarly, in conventional business, higher investment leads to higher scale of business, mostly leading to higher profit margins.

But in the financial distribution business, higher qualifications and higher investments do not necessarily result in higher earnings.

The skill and knowledge of the financial distributor and the quality or level of his or her contacts are most important in the financial distribution business.

So, as financial distribution does not require high qualification and high investments and capital, it is easier to start and scale-up.

Disadvantages of Financial Distribution Business

The financial distribution business does not require high investment. So, anybody and everybody can start at any point of time. So, there will be high competition. So, a lot of financial distributors are there in the market, claiming to be the best, leaving the client a little confused regarding who is good and who is bad.

Financial distribution business requires good knowledge of financial markets, so people not having substantial IQ, might not prosper in this business.

The financial distribution business requires regular up-gradation of knowledge. As financial markets are ever-changing, one needs to stay updated, and hence knowledge up-gradation is mandatory. So, one who is not comfortable in continuous up-gradation and training, might not prosper in this business.

As the financial distribution business does not require qualifications and investment, a lot of people end up in this business, not by choice, but by default. A lot of mediocre and below-average candidates end-up doing financial distribution business, as they did not get an alternative career opportunity. These people might end up mis-selling financial products to the client, for the sake of high commission and income, causing losses to clients, knowingly in some cases and unknowingly in some cases.

As there are a lot of operators in this business, and as there is less scope to offer product differentiation, a financial distributor needs to woo and follow up extensively, to get new business and new clients.

Thus, we can say that the financial distribution business is very competitive, as there are many market operators. Also, we can say that knowledge is very important for a financial distributor, to get established and successful in this business.

2
Important Constituents of Financial Distribution Business

The financial distribution business mainly denotes the distribution of multiple financial products under one roof. It is actually multiple businesses under one umbrella. The objective is to serve as a one-stop-solution for all clients. As margins of every business are decreasing, offering multiple products to a single client can help to increase the profitability of the financial distributor. Also, as trust factor and reliability are very important in the case of financial products, a single distributor or adviser offering multiple products, can be really convenient for the client.

Important Constituents of Financial Distribution Business :

The financial distribution business mainly comprises the following products:

1. Life Insurance – It mainly deals with a product which deals with life cover. With the help of a life insurance policy, one can protect his or her family from the financial crisis, in-case of untimely and unfortunate death.

2. Health Insurance – It is a type of insurance coverage that pays for medical, surgical, and sometimes dental expenses incurred by the insured. Health insurance claim proceeds can be reimbursed to the insured against expenses incurred by him or her, for illness or injury. Or it can be paid directly to the hospital, in-case cashless facility is available and is opted for.

3. General Insurance – It comprises of all other insurance products apart from life insurance. It comprises of all health insurance, but it has been explained separately above. It comprises of accidental insurance, car insurance, travel insurance, home insurance, burglary insurance, fire insurance, freight insurance, and many more.

4. Mutual Funds – It is a type of investment tool, through which multiple investors, with common investment objective, can invest. It is a common fund managed by an asset management company

that collects money from a number of investors who share a common investment objective. Then, it invests the money in equities, bonds, money market instruments, and/or other securities, as per the investment objective of the fund, under the supervision of a fund manager. Each investor owns units, which represent a portion of the holdings of the fund. The income/gains generated from this collective investment is distributed proportionately amongst the investors after deducting certain expenses, by calculating a scheme's "Net Asset Value" or NAV.

5. Equities and commodities – It comprise of trading in stocks (or Shares), commodities, bullion, and currency. Buying and selling of shares and commodities, generating profits or losses comprises this segment. Stock markets are seen as a barometer to an economy. And clients buying or selling stocks or commodities are known as traders. And intermediaries facilitating the trading are known as brokers or sub-brokers.

6. Loans – This is one of the most important services of the financial sector. Salaried people and individuals need loans to take care of their excess expenses, or to buy cars, or to buy homes and for many other purposes. Businessmen and business houses require loans for their businesses. Loans can be of many types. Home

loans, personal loans, car loans, and business loans are the most common type of loans.

A life insurance agent or general insurance agent or mutual fund agent or stockbroker or loan agent or a person acting as an agent of all the above products can be termed as a financial distributor. **Catering to one or a few or all the above products and services constitutes financial distribution business.**

3

Success Mantra 1
Self-Preparation

The financial distribution business does not require much capital investment initially. But self-preparation is the biggest requirement for this business. One should be properly attired. One should have proper communication skills. Also, one should always be upgrading and enhancing knowledge. Investment in one's own-self is the biggest asset of this business. One should be creating himself or herself as a brand.

(I) Role of Knowledge

Someone comes and tells me that some business school in Mumbai is very good. Coincidentally, he or she is not very much educated and does not have much knowledge about education. It is quite obvious that I will not give much importance to his or her opinion.

A lot of times, it is seen that young college students start the agency of some company, to earn some pocket money. They end up meeting the parents of their friends and try to give them some advice on investment. The parents, who might be around 45-50, might frown at the 18 years old guy or girl teaching them how and when to invest, or may just pretend to listen calmly, as he happens to be their son's or daughter's close friend. But in most probable case, they will not pay heed to his or her advice, even if it is valid advice. And this is where the role of knowledge and maturity comes into play, in the financial distribution business. If the guy or girl is having in-depth knowledge and makes a presentation in a very mature way, the prospective client might not be able to ignore, though being older in age.

A financial distributor should have an open mind to upgrade his or her knowledge in periodic intervals. Knowledge is the biggest asset of a financial distributor.

So, a financial distributor should have sound knowledge about the financial market, to be successful in this profession. Also, as maturity and experience grow with time, it becomes a valuable asset for the financial distributor. Most importantly, money, wealth and the client may be temporary, but knowledge is permanent.

(II) Perfect Mindset and Attitude

Mindset:

- Patience – To get established in the financial distribution business, a lot of patience is required. Clients start with small business, to test the knowledge and reliability of a financial distributor. Then gradually business volume increases. Then clients increase as references from satisfied clients start coming in.

- Perseverance – A lot of perseverance is required to be a successful financial distributor. A financial distributor has to follow-up very strongly to close a deal. A financial distributor should have a mindset of not giving up easily. The financial distributor should have the persistence and tenacity, to keep following up with the client till the end, even if it's hard.

- Humility – The financial distributor, however big he or she is, should never be arrogant. He should always approach the client with politeness and humility.

- Honesty – The financial distributor should be honest and true in his or her transactions with the client.

- Transparency – The financial distributor should be transparent while discussing with the client, the benefits and risks of a client.

- Mutual Win-Win Approach – The financial distributor, should always try to give priority to clients' benefits and interests. The financial distributor should not only think about their own benefit. He or she should think about his or her benefit, only after ensuring the benefit of the client.

Attitude:

- Be a Listener – A financial distributor should be a good listener. He or she should listen to the requirements and needs of the client, and address them while giving the suggested solution.

- Open to Learning – A financial distributor should always be willing to learn about new trends and practices and try to implement them.

- Friendly – A financial distributor should be friendly in nature while interacting with the client. If he or she is always very serious and formal while interacting with the client, the client might not feel very comfortable. So financial distributor should try to be friendly with the client, to establish better rapport and understanding.

- Proactive - Good financial distributors keep the lines of communication open, updating the clients on current financial issues and opportunities. They help to make complex financial concepts easy to understand. A good financial distributor needs to be proactive, needs to take prompt initiatives to connect with new clients, and seek opportunities for business closure.

- Socialising – A financial distributor needs to socialise well to be successful. A financial distributor needs new prospects, every day, every-week and every-month. And these new prospects can be sourced through parties, get-togethers, and meet-ups.

- Disciplined – A financial distributor needs to be disciplined. He or she needs to devote time regularly or consistently for this business. Ideally, a full timer should meet 2-3 prospects per day. And a part-timer should meet 6-8 new prospects every week. And this should be practised regularly and consistently. Also, a financial distributor should ensure that he or she attends every client's appointments at the exact time. Punctuality helps to create a good impression in the mind of the client.

- More Humane Interaction – The interaction between the client and financial distributor should be more humane in nature. The discussion should not only constitute of technical jargon. The discussion should be such, that the client is able to connect with the financial distributor.

(III) Perfect Appearance and Body Language

Appearance:

Well-Dressed – The financial distributor should go on client appointments well dressed. The financial distributor should ideally go on client meetings in formal attire and should avoid casuals during meetings.

Confident – The financial distributor should look confident, at the time of client meetings and presentations. He or she should not fumble, or look confused, in front of the clients.

Body Language:

Body language is a very important part of any business interaction. It creates a very important impact on the result of any meeting.

The following tips should be maintained:

- Maintain good eye contact.

- Ensure proper face to face interaction.

- Have a nice smile.

- Ensure warm handshake.

- Avoid excessive movement (Don't fidget).

- Keep an open body stance (Don't have folded hands while interacting).

- Make use of gestures while talking.

- Learn to use your voice (Practise proper tone/ voice modulation).

- Avoid invading client's space (Maintain a distance of around 3 feet from the client).

4

Success Mantra 2

Enquiry Generation

Develop contacts, do constant networking, and keep prospecting. It is like oxygen for this business. Anyone and everyone can be a prospect. But one needs to constantly keep adding new client-base.

(I) Role of Contacts

Mr. Sachin Tendulkar is personally known to me.

Mr. Amitabh Bachchan is personally known to me.

And Mr. Sachin Tendulkar is not personally known to me.

And Mr. Amitabh Bachchan is not personally known to me.

What is the difference?

What is the probability of Mr. Sachin Tendulkar or Mr. Amitabh Bachchan becoming my client, and doing investment through me?

What is the amount or volume of business that Mr. Sachin Tendulkar or Mr. Amitabh Bachchan can be giving me?

If Mr. Sachin Tendulkar or Mr. Amitabh Bachchan is personally known to me, there is a high probability that they can do transactions through me. And if they do the transaction through me, they have the potential to give me a high volume of business. So, there is a high probability that can give me a good volume of business. Also, they can give me repeat business. And if I can satisfy them, there is a high probability that they can refer me to clients of high potential, which can translate to a higher volume of business.

But if Mr. Sachin Tendulkar or Mr. Amitabh Bachchan is not known to me there is almost zero probability that I will get business through them.

So, we can say that a good contact base is a major key to success in the financial distribution business. But without good contacts also, one can do a financial distribution business, but the growth will be slower. And a person having good contacts can grow very faster in this business.

(II) Role of Relationship

My friend listens blindly to me.

My friend listens to me but also questions me at times.

My friend always questions me.

In the above three cases, what is the probability that my friend will do transactions through me, and give me business?

If my friend listens blindly to me, there is a high probability that my friend will take all my advices, and do major investments through me.

So, the amount and ease of business that a financial distributor can do with a client is fully proportional to the level of rapport, the distributor enjoys with the client.

Most financial distributors, on an attempt to complete sales targets, make the mistake of trying to sell to the client on the first visit itself. But this should not be the case.

If there is no relationship between the distributor and client there is a high probability that the distributor will not get any business from the prospective client.

So, a financial distributor, in the initial days should approach people, with whom, he or she shares a good relationship.

And in case of a new or unknown client, a distributor should try to establish a good relationship or rapport with the client, before pitching for any product or sacrifices.

So, the relationship is one of the most important pillars in the financial distribution business.

A client hands over his or her savings to the distributor for its growth. To do so, the client needs to have a high level of trust in the distributor. And this trust comes only with a good relationship and rapport.

So, a financial distributor should firstly focus on establishing a good relationship with a prospective client before trying to do business with the client.

(III) Prospecting

Prospecting is the backbone of any business. Every business need sales.

And sales are dependent on prospecting.

But what is prospecting ?

Prospecting is the first step in the sales process, which consists of identifying potential customers. The objective of prospecting is to develop a list of likely customers and then systematically following up with them in the hopes of converting them from potential customers to current customers.

Eight Sources of Prospecting :

- Personal References – Every Individual has personal acquaintances. Relatives, friends, neighbours can be prospective clients. But at first, the list needs to be screened before prospecting.

  Some close contacts, instead of giving business, might try to create a negative influence. These types of people should be avoided.

  Some close contacts, might not be able to give direct business, but can recommend to big clients. These contacts need to be approached accordingly.

- Cold Calls –This is a process wherein you connect to unknown people who have not made any query. It works on the concept of probability. Say 100 unknown people are approached, maybe 10 people could be converted as new client.

- Qualified Leads – These are a list of people who had made some enquiries, through some website, portal, or digital campaign. The leads acquired are then followed up for prospecting and converting to new clients. Normally conversion ratio is higher in the case of qualified leads than cold calls.

- Client References – References and recommendations by satisfied clients can also be used for prospecting. In this type of prospecting, the conversion ratio is normally higher.

- Trade Fairs & Events – These sorts of promotional events help in generating leads which can be used for prospecting. All visitors visiting and enquiring at these events may be treated as qualified leads. Chances of conversions are also higher in these cases.

- Social Media – Nowadays lot of people can be connected through social platforms like Facebook, LinkedIn, etc. Products and services can be promoted in these social platforms and leads can be generated, which can be used for prospecting.

- Networking – Nowadays networking, connecting to people has become easier. Networking can be done through a lot of networking associations like BNI (Business Network International), JCI (Junior Chamber International), Lions, Rotary. And these connections can be easily used for prospecting.

- Old Clients – It is also a good source of prospecting. Old clients, lost clients, old leads can always be used for fresh prospecting. And there are chances of freshly converting these leads and clients.

So prospecting is a very important part of the financial distribution business. A financial distributor, should keep on prospecting, and never end the process, to keep growing in this business.

(IV) Getting Appointments

This is the most difficult part of this business when it comes to getting new clients. Talking to an unknown client, and getting an appointment to meet is not that easy.

Script 1: "Hello, I am Mr ABC calling from XYZ Co. I would like to meet you regarding investment matters."

Probable Responses:

Response 1: Bang. Hangs up the Call.

Response 2: "I am not interested."

Response 3: "From where did you get my phone number."

Response 4: "Please don't disturb."

Script 2:

Caller: "Hello, Am I speaking to Mr. Z ?"

Prospect: "Yes !"

Caller: "Is this the right time to talk to you ?"

Prospect: "Regarding what ?"

Caller: "I am Mr ABC calling from XYZ Co. I got your number from ……. I am working in the financial markets since ……. I would like to meet and discuss with you regarding certain new concepts."

Prospect: "You can brief me over the phone."

Caller: "Sorry Sir, everything cannot be briefed over the phone. It is best to discuss this across the table. I will not take much of your time. I am sure the discussion will be of immense benefit to you."

Prospect: "But I am very busy. And I am not willing to invest anything."

Caller: "It is necessary for only busy and successful people like you. And you don't need to invest anything now. I will discuss certain new concepts with you. If you like the concept, then we can take forward our discussions, else we can drop further discussions. Can I come down on a *Date & Time* to meet you? I will not take more than 15-20 minutes of your valuable time."

Prospect: "Ok"

Remember, try to be courteous over the phone. Modulate your voice accordingly. And never try to sell any product or solution over the phone.

5

Success Mantra 3
Effective Conversion

The success of this business depends on the presentation and closing. One should give solutions and not products. And one should do proper need analysis and portfolio review before suggesting anything.

(I) Meeting and Giving Presentations

After getting an appointment from a client, next comes the most vital task. Meeting the client and trying to convince him or her.

Remember first impression is the last impression.

Ways to create a good first impression: -

- Dress appropriately.

- Be on time.

- Do right handshake.

- Have proper eye contact.

- Have a nice smile.

- Have a positive attitude/mindset.

- Look confident and professional.

- Have a memorable introduction.

- Try to create some rapport by discussing casual topics, before getting into the main topic or presentation.

- Be a good listener.

- Do proper home-work before meeting the client.

- Try to address client's pain points.

Ways of opening a conversation:

- Through Question

  - Your drawing room is very nice. Did you do it on your own or did you hire some interior designer? Are the designs and items chosen by you? Or your wife?

  - Connect the above to the need for financial planning. Ask the client, "Don't you feel, to have a nice home with a well-decorated drawing room, you need proper financial planning."

> ➤ Can you guess what can be the cost of an MBA Course at IIM after 15 years?

> Connect the above to the need for financial planning. Ask the client, "Don't you feel, to plan for your child's higher education, you need proper financial planning."

> ➤ Can you guess what can be the cost of rice per kg, when you retire?

> Connect the above to the need for financial planning. Ask the client, "Don't you feel, to plan for your retirement, you need proper financial planning."

> ➤ What is your dream?

> Connect the above to the need for financial planning. Ask the client, "Don't you feel, to achieve your dream, you need proper financial planning."

- Through a Case Study

> ➤ Last week I had met a client who had 19 life insurance policies, which he wanted me to review. I had gone through his policies and told him which was good for him and which was not.

> ➢ Last month, I had met a friend of mine who just got married. He wanted to start some savings for his family. I was glad to guide him, and he was very happy, realising that starting early would really be helpful for him.

Types of Presentations:

- **Product Based Presentation** - This sort of presentation mainly deals with specific products. Mainly it deals with the product features. In this case, normally, the product is suggested even before need analysis. This is not very preferable.

- **Concept Based Presentation** – This sort of presentation deals with concepts and ideas which relate to client's daily life.

Few examples:

> ➢ Maybe explaining the need of airbag or stepney (Extra Tyre) and relating it to the need of insurance and savings.

> ➢ Or maybe explaining the role of a wrapper to a chocolate, and comparing it to the need for insurance and savings.

> ➢ Or maybe explaining the role of an antivirus in a computer, and comparing it to the need for insurance and savings.

> ➢ Or maybe explaining the role of research and planning while buying a home, and comparing it to the need for financial planning.

- **Solution Based Presentation** – This sort of presentation deals with solutions that the clients might be looking for, and then relating to products. Say, explaining the need for retirement planning or child planning, and then relating it to some product or combination of products.

(II) Objection Handling

Common Objections:

- Don't have time to meet

  > ➢ Why are we all working ? To have a great future ! And for a better future, we need proper planning. What do you say ?
  >
  > If I take 15-20 minutes of yours, from your busy schedule, to help you to plan a better future, will it be a big loss ?

- I have already done my planning

  > ➢ For any medical problem, don't you ever go for a second opinion ? Similarly, there is no harm in taking a second opinion and reviewing your existing plan or portfolio.

- I don't have money to invest

  - The question of investing immediately does not arise. We need to first review your portfolio. Maybe some reshuffling might be required, which does not require fresh investment. Only in case, there is some shortage to achieve some financial goal, the new investment might be required. But it may also be the case that your existing plan is perfect, and no further investment is required.

- I will invest in my business as it gives higher returns.

  - There are two forms of investment – active and passive. Investment in business is active investment where active participation is required to generate returns. Investment in financial instruments is passive investment, where active participation is not required. Fund managers and portfolio managers are responsible for generating returns.

- Return in previous investments are Low

  - If one meets with an accident, one will not move out of the house ? Yes, one needs to be careful. Similarly, if someone has burnt his or her fingers in the past while investing, one needs to be careful in future investments and planning.

- My tax savings is complete

  - Is tax exemption the only reason for financial planning ? Getting exemptions under section 80C or 80D should not be the only objective for financial planning. The main objective of financial planning is to achieve future financial goals.

- I have sufficient insurance

  - In case if you are not there tomorrow, will your family get the necessary amount from your existing policies. If you don't know, you need to calculate at the earliest. And if it is not sufficient, you need to add your insurance cover.

- I need to consult my chartered accountant

  - You can always consult your chartered accountant. But that does not stop us from discussing. You can then compare and decide what is best for you.

- Equity linked investments are risky

  - No risk - No gain. One needs to keep a portion of the investment in equity linked products, to get higher returns in the long term.

- Guaranteed schemes offer less returns

  - ➢ Obviously, guaranteed schemes will give lower returns. Because there are no risk factors associated with it. One needs to understand that one cannot keep 100% investments in equity linked products.

- Bank fixed deposits are better

  - ➢ It is obviously good. One should keep a portion of fixed deposits for emergency requirements. It gives the necessary liquidity at the time of emergency. But one needs to understand that returns from fixed deposit are taxable. Also, it has reinvestment risk, at the time of renewing a fixed deposit, which arises due to a falling rate of interest.

- PPF is better

  - ➢ It is obviously good. But there is a certain lock-in period. And there is no guarantee of the interest rate. It gets declared every year, and the rate of interest might gradually decrease in the coming years.

- Don't want to lock in the funds

  - ➢ Without locking the investment for a specific period, good returns can never be generated. To get higher returns from equity markets, investment needs to be kept for 7-10 Years.

And in the case of debt products, one can get a fixed rate of return for a longer period, if the investment is locked for a longer period.

A financial distributor should always acknowledge client objections, and try to address it, instead of denying the fact that the client might be having certain objections.

(III) Sales Propositions

This is the most important part of closing deal in a financial distribution business.

One needs to identify edge/niche/unique features that one can offer to the client.

Easy Ways to do so:

- Identify pain points a client would like to avoid –

  - ➢ Say a client is disturbed for not getting reminders for insurance premium renewals.

  - ➢ Say the client is unhappy about the claim settlement of the existing Mediclaim policy.

  - ➢ Say a client is disturbed for being suggested mutual funds which has not given profits.

  - ➢ Say the client is unhappy for not being properly educated about the risk factors of the investment schemes.

  - ➢ Say a client is unhappy for being charged high brokerage in the share trading account.

The financial distributor should ensure or assure the client that the client will not face these problems if the client avails his or her services.

- Identify pleasures a client might want –

  - Say a client wants low risk.

  - Say a client wants higher returns.

  - Say a client wants transparency.

  - Say a client wants door step service.

  - Say a client wants customised advice and solution.

    The financial distributor should ensure or assure the client that the client will get all the above if the client avails his or her services.

- Identify edge/USPs of different products offered –

  - Say a life insurance term plan comes with joint life option.

  - Say a health insurance comes with global coverage.

  - Say a mutual fund comes with an ATM card and 100% liquidity anytime, with zero exit load.

> ➤ Say a trading account comes with brokerage per trade.

> ➤ Say a car insurance comes with a bumper-to-bumper option.

> The financial distributor should highlight the above USPs in front of the client, to convince them to go for the above products, through him or her.

(IV) Need Analysis

This is a very important part of financial distribution business and financial planning.

A 45-year-old male having 2 children, one son of 8 years and a daughter of 6 years, will need to save money for future, for children's education and marriage. But a 65-years-old male, having a single daughter, who was married 10 years ago, will not have the same need.

A 45-year-old single lady, having a dependant mother, and a home loan of 50 lakhs, will need to take protection, in case of untimely death so that her home loan gets paid off from the life insurance proceeds, and also there remains some surplus, to take care of her mother's need.

Important Aspects of Need Analysis

- **Human Life Value**

  It is the present value of all future income that one could expect to earn for one's family. It is defined as the total income an individual is expected to earn until retirement. It indicates the economic loss a family would suffer in case of the early demise of the earning member.

  Step One: Estimate the insured's remaining lifetime earnings, taking into consideration both the "average" annual salary and potential future increases.

  Step Two: Subtract a reasonable estimate of annual income taxes and living expenses. As a rule of thumb, this figure should be close to about 70% of the income, although this number may vary from family to family, depending on individual budgets.

  Step Three: Determine the length of time for which earnings will need to be replaced. This time period could be until the insured's dependents are fully grown, and no longer require financial support, or until the insured's assumed retirement age.

Step Four: Select a discount rate for future earnings. A conservative figure for this estimate could be the assumed rate of return on bank fixed deposit.

Step Five: Multiply the net salary needed by the length of time needed to determine the future earnings. Then, using the assumed rate of return, figure out the present value of future earnings.

- **Time Value of Money**

The time value of money (TVM) is the concept that money you have now is worth more than the identical sum in the future due to its potential earning capacity. This core principle of finance holds that provided money can earn interest, any amount of money is worth more the sooner it is received. TVM is also sometimes referred to as present discounted value.

The time value of money is based on the idea that people would rather have money today than in the future.

Given that money can earn compound interest, it is more valuable in the present rather than the future.

The formula for the computing time value of money considers the payment now, the future value, the interest rate, and the time frame.

In general, the most fundamental TVM formula takes into account the following variables:

FV = Future value of money

PV = Present value of money

R = Interest rate

T = Number of years

Based on the above variables, the formula for TVM are as below:

FV = PV x [1 + (R/100) ^ T]

PV = FV / [1 + (R/100) ^ T]

- **A Practical Example**

Need analysis of a 45 year old male person, whose spouse is housewife, and son is 8 years old, who is working in a firm and drawing an annual salary of Rupees 5 Lakhs.

- Assume retirement age of the client to be 60 Years Age.

- Assume current year expense to be 70% of current annual salary.

- Assume current annual inflation at 5%

- Assume annual salary increment at 4%

- Assume current annual bank rate of interest at 6%

- **The Solution**

AGE	YEAR	PROJECTED SALARY	PROJECTED EXPENSE	CURRENT VALUE OF EXPENSES
45	0	500000	350000	350000
46	1	520000	367500	346698
47	2	540800	385875	343427
48	3	562432	405169	340187
49	4	584929	425427	336978
50	5	608326	446699	333799
51	6	632660	469033	330650
52	7	657966	492485	327531
53	8	684285	517109	324441
54	9	711656	542965	321380
55	10	740122	570113	318348
56	11	769727	598619	315345
57	12	800516	628550	312370
58	13	832537	659977	309423
59	14	865838	692976	306504
60	15	900472	727625	303612
TOTAL CURRENT HUMAN LIFE VALUE				**5220695**

Thus, it is very important that the financial distributor use certain tools, and calculations to determine the needs of the client, before suggesting any solution. So, the financial distributor should use different scientific and logical processes and calculate how much life insurance or health insurance or retirement corpus or child education corpus maybe required by the client, before suggesting any solution.

This helps the financial distributor in gaining the trust of the client and thereby establishing a long-term relationship with the client and his or her family.

(V) Portfolio Review

This is another very important aspect of financial distribution business and financial planning.

And this is the area which most financial distributors also ignore. Sometimes due to ignorance and sometimes in hurry to sell new products or solutions.

Also, sometimes clients are unwilling to share information regarding past investments.

In both cases, where the distributer or planner ignores past investments, and where the client suppresses past investment, the practice is wrong. It is something like a doctor prescribing medicine to a patient, without knowing whether the client has any previous allergy to any specific group of medicines.

Ideally, a financial distributor or adviser or planner first should enquire about the clients existing investments, plans, and investment habits, before suggesting any new solutions.

Once I had met a client through some reference. It was the first meeting. So, the client first asked "What do you do?" I said, "I review existing Investments and suggest what to do on that basis." On listening to my reply, the client invited me to his house the next day to review his investments. I still remember, once I reached your house, he handed me 19 life insurance policies, few running, few lapsed. On reviewing those, I first observed, he didn't have a term insurance and health insurance. So, I suggested him to first take a term insurance and health insurance. Then I suggested him to continue few policies and discontinue few policies. Then I suggested a retirement plan, as he did not have one. Today he is a satisfied client of mine. He has recommended me to a lot of his friends and relatives, and they are also my satisfied client.

Had I approached the above client directly with some product or solution, without portfolio review, I don't think I could have converted the client. Thus, a portfolio review is important from the point of view of both the client and the financial distributor. The client is benefited as a review is done, and also feels good, that someone is reviewing his or her investment or financial planning for the benefit of the client. Also, the distributor is benefited, as he or she might get new business if there is some deficit in the existing planning.

So a financial distributor or planner should always first do a portfolio review before suggesting any new product or solution.

(VI) Solutions Based Approach of Financial Planning

Financial planning and financial distribution are inter-linked. Financial distribution business without knowledge of financial planning has no future in the current scenario.

A financial distributor, having no knowledge about financial planning, will go to clients soliciting to take different financial products, and will be seen by the client as a common **"Agent"** or **"Broker"**.

A financial distributor, having knowledge about financial planning, will never go to clients soliciting to take different financial products. He or she will be giving solutions to clients, and will be respected by the client as an **"Adviser"** or **"Consultant"**.

So ideally, a financial distributor should go to the client with concepts and solutions.

Common solutions that form a part of financial planning–

1.   **Solution**

➤   In case you die, your family gets protected from financial uncertainty.

Product - Life Insurance

2.   **Solution**

> In case you or your family members get hospitalised, your hospital bills are paid off.

Product - Health Insurance

3.   **Solution**

> When your child grows up and goes to college, his or her college expenses are taken care of.

Product - Child Planning

4.   **Solution**

> When you grow old and retire, your regular expenses are taken care of.

Product - Retirement Planning

5.   **Solution**

> If you are planning to purchase a flat or bungalow, your fund requirement is taken care of.

Product - Home Loan

Strangely the client might not be liking the product like "Life Insurance" but likes the concept of "Family Protection" and hence might end up giving consent to buying a term insurance.

So financial distributors and advisers are suggested to approach the clients, with a certain attractive concept or solution, instead of approaching them with some specific product.

(VII) Telling Stories and adding Emotions

Storytelling has been popular always, but nowadays it has become a very important mode even in business communication.

Normal Pitch:

Good morning, Sir, I am a financial distributor. Recently XYZ Company, for which I am working, has launched ABC product. It is a very good child plan. Why don't you have a look at it?

Story Telling Pitch:

Good morning Sir! How are you? How is your son doing? He reads in which class?

(Client says class 2)

Oh nice. I met a client yesterday. His son also studies in class 2. He was very worried about his son's future. He wanted guaranteed tax free 2 crore after 20 years. I suggested a new product ABC of XYZ company. He was very happy, and he gave a cheque of 5 Lakhs yesterday only.

Normal Pitch:

Good morning, Sir ! I am a financial distributor. I help you to review your existing investments.

Story Telling Pitch:

Good morning, Sir ! How are you ? How do you normally do your investments ? You prefer to invest in guaranteed or equity linked products ? Yesterday I had visited one client. He had 19 life insurance policies. A few were running and few lapsed. He was very confused. I helped him to sort out the policies and he is very happy. Similarly, I can also help you re-organise your existing investments.

Remember to add emotions to the stories. Emphasise on children future, family protection as normally clients are emotional regarding these points.

(VIII) Closing Deals

Emphasise the Need: After giving a presentation, the need from the client's point of view needs to be emphasised. First make the client agree to the proposition, and agree that he or she needs the solution.

Emphasise the effect of Delay:

Client – I agree that I need the solution. Let's do it in the coming month.

Adviser – Can you predict what is in store for tomorrow?

In case Insurance is suggested -

I had met a client in october. He agreed that he will take a term insurance and health insurance in november. But unfortunately, in october end, he was diagnosed to have cancer. And he couldn't be given any insurance.

In case Debt Product is suggested –

There are high chances of a rate cut in the coming month. In that case, the rate of interest will fall. And you might loose on the returns.

In case Equity Product is suggested –

In case the market rises from here, you might end up buying at higher levels. And you might not get the expected returns.

Offer some Extra Benefit–

In the coming month, all my existing clients and I are going for a weekend Singapore trip at a very subsidised cost, as our number of members is over 100, and the tour operator is also my client. So, if you become my client today, maybe you could also join along-with your family, at an unimaginable price.

From the coming month, term insurance premiums are going to rise. So, if you complete the formalities now, you will get it at a much cheaper cost.

In this month, there are certain waivers on the medicals for health insurance. So, if you complete the formalities now, you might get your health insurance, with minimum medicals.

6
Success Mantra 4
Enhancing Relationships

Developing relationships and rapport with clients is very important in this business. One needs to keep constant engagement with existing clients. One should look forward to referrals and recommendations. Also, one should try to connect with influencers. And look forward to selling opportunities.

(I) Up-selling

This is one of the easiest jobs if the proper relationship is maintained with existing clients. The entire finance business is dependent on *trust*. And if clients are given proper solutions and after-sales service, *trust factor* keeps increasing.

So, if a financial distributor or adviser has the full trust of the client, and is able to understand the needs of the client, it is very easy to upsell.

The client will not have the same requirements lifelong. Say a client gets married. Or gets a promotion. Or there is a new child in the family. So, there will be a need for more insurance. There will be a need for more savings. So, if the financial distributor or adviser is well connected with the client, up-selling is very easily possible in this case.

The best way to up-sell is to make the client realise that there is a real need for increasing the protection or savings to take care of the enhanced financial goals.

Also, it should always be presented in such a way, that the client feels that the financial distributor or adviser is very concerned about the client's wellbeing.

And it should never be presented in such a way, that the client feels that the financial distributor or adviser is trying to sell some additional financial products for extra commission income.

(II) Client Engagement

Client engagement is very important for the financial distribution business.

Client engagement does not always mean business, but without engagement, a business cannot happen.

We normally meet a client, or look forward to new clients, with the expectation of new business. But it does not mean, we should forget the client after we get the business.

Benefits of Engaging:

- Creating good connect and rapport with the client.

- Get repeated business in due course of time.

- Get references for new probable clients, from existing clients.

Ways of Engaging:

- Wishing on birthdays and anniversaries.

- Giving calendars during new year or gifts during Diwali.

- Inviting in social events or get-togethers.

- Periodically updating the clients about the current market scenario.

Remember one old proverb, "Out of Sight, Out of Mind".

If you stop engaging with a very loyal client also, there may come one day, your client might say, "Hey! I just forgot about you, as we had not been in touch for quite long, I just took a new life insurance policy from my bank relationship manager, as I needed to increase my term insurance coverage.

(III) Referrals

Referrals are one of the important resources for the growth of a financial distribution business.

Some people might debate that approaching references are like cold calls. But the reality is that in some cases, references work very well. And in some cases, it is worse than cold calls. There are a lot of reasons behind such a wide difference in the effectiveness. To ensure that the references work effectively, the following points need to be ensured.

Referrals need to be asked from good clients only. A good client will give reference to good prospects. It is normally expected that a good person will have a good social circle.

Referrals need to be asked from clients and at a proper time. Say a distributor has met a client for the first or second time to discuss some plan, and the distributor asks for references, the client will never be comfortable to give any reference. And even if he or she gives some reference out of courtesy, it will never be effective. Because the distributor has not gained the trust of the client, and so the client will never want to refer the distributor to his or her close friends and relatives.

Referrals need to be given in a proper way to be effective. Sometimes clients gives few names and numbers and tell not to mention the name of the client as the referrer. In that case, approaching those references will be worse than a cold call. The client should give reference to his close friend or relative, to whom the distributor can mention the name of the client as the referrer. Also, the client should mention a brief background of the reference, so that the distributor can do some homework before approaching the reference for an appointment.

Referrals work downwards and not upwards. Say a security guard in an office gives the name and contact number of the CEO of the company, it can never be treated as a reference, because the CEO will never be willing to discuss financial matters with a financial distributor, who has been referred by his security guard. But if the Zonal Head of an organisation refers a financial distributor to some Branch Head in his direct team, the Branch Head might be highly delighted to take the advice of the financial distributor, as he might be having high respect for his Zonal Head, for his financial decisions.

(IV) Recommendations

Recommendations are another important resource for the growth of a financial distribution business.

Recommendations are obviously more effective than referrals.

Recommendations should only be sought from selective clients. One financial distributor needs to decide, with which clients he or she is comfortable to work. Suppose there is a client, who might have given some small business, but is very fussy. The distributor has to decide whether he or she is comfortable working with the client. In case the distributor is not comfortable to work with the client, the distributor should not ask for recommendations from the client. The distributor should only seek recommendations from clients, with whom he or she is comfortable to work with.

Recommendations also need to be asked by clients at a proper time. One financial distributor should ask his or client to recommend to the client's contact sphere, i.e., friends, relatives, and colleagues, ideally after 2-3 years of close association.

Recommendations should be done in the way one wants, and in the way that one wants to brand himself or herself. The distributor should decide, how he or she wants the client to introduce the distributor to the client's contact base. The distributor might want to be introduced as "Financial Consultant" or "Financial Expert" or "Insurance Agent" or "Financial Planner". The distributor needs to decide and brief the clients accordingly. Also, the distributor should insist on the client to personally talk to the prospects, and recommend in a very favourable manner.

The Client might recommend in the following manner, "Meet Mr. X, my financial adviser. You may contact him for your financial needs."

Also, the client might recommend in the following manner, "Meet Mr. X, my financial adviser. He has been advising me for the last 5 years. He has guided me very nicely all throughout. I have got very good service from him. He also has very good knowledge of the financial markets. So, you may also consult him for all your financial needs, and I believe you will be benefited."

The second way of recommendation will be always more effective.

Recommendations work best when the client takes personal interest or initiative in introducing to the prospective client.

(V) Influencers

Influencers are another important resource for the growth of a financial distribution business.

It is like a catalyst in a chemical reaction. Influencers are really helpful in getting business faster.

Say a financial distributor is targeting to give term insurance to labourers in a factory. The normal process is that one needs to go and meet the labourers individually and convince them. But imagine the labour union leader is a close friend of the financial distributor. If the labour union leader tells all the labourers that term insurance is very useful, and everyone should take one life insurance policy, there is high scope of conversion. Further, if the labour union leader recommends his friend to the labourers, the trust factor increases, and there is a higher scope of conversion.

Say a financial distributor is targeting to give health insurance to members of a specific church. The normal process is that one needs to go to the church and meet the members individually and convince them. But imagine the Father of the church is a close friend of the financial distributor. If the father of the church tells all the members that health insurance is very useful, and everyone should take one health insurance policy, there is high scope of conversion.

So, every financial distributor should try to identify probable Influencers, in his or her contact-sphere, to fast track his or her business.

7

Success Mantra 5
Honesty and Integrity

Maintaining ethical values and giving proper after sales service is very vital in the financial distribution business. Also never forget or ignore the client after the sales is complete. And be transparent and honest with clients, to ensure continuous loyalty.

(I) After Sales Service

This is another very important aspect of financial distribution business and financial planning.

Maximum financial distributors stop giving service, or give poor service, or stop communication with the clients after one sales deal gets closed.

What happens, as a result, the dissatisfied client keeps blaming the entire fraternity of financial distributors and planners. Whenever a new distributor or planner visits or connects with the specific client, the client sees the distributor or planner with an eye of suspicion.

Also, the distributor, by not giving proper after-sales services, loses out on future business and possibilities of references and recommendations from the client.

If a financial distributor gives proper service, there are high chances of getting references and recommendations from clients. But if the financial distributor does not give proper service, clients will never want to refer him or her to friends and relatives.

So a financial distributor or planner should try to give the best possible after-sales service to all clients. After sales service is the biggest pillar of the financial distribution business.

(II) Ethical Values

All other business requires ethical values for long term growth and goodwill. But the financial distribution business requires ethical values the most, as financial distribution business revolves around money. And dealings with money require trust, honesty and transparency.

A client trusts the financial distributor or planner, with his or her hard-earned money. So, if the financial distributor or planner is not reliable, the client will never want to trust the financial distributor.

Apart from being knowledgeable, the financial distributor needs to be reliable, to get business from clients. Financial distributors maintaining high ethical values runs business life long, and even the business gets carried on for generations.

If a financial distributor is reliable and trustworthy, there are high chances of getting references and recommendations from clients. But if the financial distributor does not maintain ethics, clients will never want to refer him or her to friends and relatives.

In case of a lot of life insurance agents and stockbrokers who are carrying on the business today, the original business was started by their grandfathers. This means that they have maintained high ethical values over generations, and have gained the trust of the clients.

Also, there are some life insurance agents, who take premiums in cash from clients, but do not deposit the same to the Life Insurance Corporation office. These sort of dishonest agents or distributors, get wiped out of the financial industry, within a very short span of time.

So, a financial distributor needs to maintain high ethical values to successful in this business and gain a reputation and trust among clients.

8

Common Mistakes that Distributors should avoid

1. Treating financial distributorship as a common sales job and going to clients to sell some financial products, without understanding even the need of the client, before pitching any product or solution.

2. Not recognising the need for knowledge and communication skills required for the financial distribution business.

3. Under-estimating smaller clients. Normally everyone is looking for HNI clients. But smaller clients are easier to convince and if the number of clients is more, smaller clients can also generate a good volume of business.

4. Having a generalised approach. Offering the same product or solution to most of the clients might turn out to be counter-productive. Today's clients are highly educated and informed, and they look for customised solutions.

Conclusion

Indian financial markets have still not matured. Most Indian financial advisers and distributors are also not very skilled to advice their existing clients. Also, they lack the knowledge and expertise, that is necessary to get new clients.

The objective of this book is to up-skill the financial advisers to be successful in this profession, so that they can advise their clients well. Also some techniques have been discussed.

By writing this book, I hope I have been able to progress to a certain extent in my mission. But my mission and efforts to up-skill the financial adviser and distributor community will continue.

NOTES:

NOTES:

NOTES:

NOTES:

9 789390 463558